Preparing for the SHRM-CP® Exam 2026/27

Third Edition

PREPARING FOR THE SHRM-CP® EXAM 2026/27

THE OFFICIAL WORKBOOK AND PRACTICE QUESTIONS FROM SHRM

THIRD EDITION

Editors: Charles Glover, MS, Director,
Certification and Assessment Products, SHRM,
and Hanna Evans, MPS, SHRM-CP, Manager,
HR Certification and Assessment Products, SHRM

First published in the United States and Great Britain in 2026 by Kogan Page Limited

Society for Human Resources Management (SHRM)
SHRM, Alexandria, Virginia, shrm.org
SHRM, India Office, Mumbai, India, shrm.org/in
SHRM, Middle East and North Africa Office, Dubai, UAE, shrm.org/mena

Kogan Page
Kogan Page Ltd., 2nd Floor, 45 Gee Street, London EC1V 3RS, United Kingdom
Kogan Page Inc., 8 W 38th Street, Suite 902, New York, NY 10018, USA
www.koganpage.com

EU Representative (GPSR)
eucomply OÜ, Pärnu mnt 139b–14 11317, Tallinn, Estonia
www.eucompliancepartner.com

Kogan Page books are printed on paper from sustainable forests.

ISBNs
Paperback 9781398627741
Ebook 9781398627758

Library of Congress Cataloguing-in-Publication Data
A CIP record for this book is available from the Library of Congress.

British Library Cataloguing-in-Publication Data
A CIP record for this book is available from the British Library.

Typeset by Hong Kong FIVE Workshop, Hong Kong

Contents

APPENDIX 1

APPENDIX 2

Acknowledgments

This workbook was made possible by the thoughtful and generous advice, guidance, and input of many smart and talented subject matter experts, especially the following:

Mike Aitken, executive vice president, members and communities, SHRM

Alexander Alonso, PhD, SHRM-SCP, chief knowledge officer, SHRM

Nicholas Schacht, SHRM-SCP, product development and events, SHRM

Nancy Woolever, MAIS, SHRM-SCP, vice president, academic and student communities, SHRM

Sarah Chuon, SHRM-CP, specialist, exam development, SHRM

Giselle Calliste, SHRM-CP, specialist, exam development, SHRM

Jasmine Bell, SHRM-CP, specialist, exam development, SHRM

Sampoorna Nandi, PhD, sr specialist, certification and assessment products, SHRM

We also gratefully acknowledge the scores of SHRM members, SHRM certificate holders, and exam candidates who provided input for this book.

Introduction

We applaud your decision to move your career in Human Resources forward by pursuing a certification with SHRM! To this end, this workbook is designed to help you prepare for the **SHRM Certified Professional (SHRM-CP©)** exam.

Specifically, the SHRM-CP exam is designed to determine who has the level of competency and knowledge that is expected for HR professionals who perform (or will perform) operational work. This includes such duties as implementing policies, serving as the HR point of contact, performing day-to-day HR functions, and much more.

In this third edition, we continue to place great emphasis on utilizing and understanding the SHRM Body of Applied Skills and Knowledge (SHRM BASK®)—bridging the knowledge, concepts, and competencies that the SHRM BASK encapsulates to the SHRM-CP exams. Perhaps most importantly, this workbook includes a total of 25 practice items that were used on past SHRM-CP exams. These practice items will provide you with more exposure to the types of items that you will see on the real exam, as well as feedback about correct responses. These items were not simply created for this book—they were taken from actual SHRM-CP exams that were used in previous years.

On the other hand, the SHRM Senior Certified Professional (SHRM-SCP) designation is for HR professionals who are advanced in their careers. This level of professional primarily works in a strategic role, such as developing policies and strategies, overseeing the execution of integrated HR operations, directing the entire HR enterprise, and leading the alignment of HR strategies to organizational goals. Although the SHRM-CP and SHRM-SCP exams are very similar in structure, this workbook is focused exclusively on the SHRM-CP exam.

It is important to note that this workbook is designed to be used along with the official SHRM study guide: *Ace Your SHRM Certification Exam: The Official SHRM Study Guide for the SHRM-CP and SHRM-SCP Exams*, the SHRM BASK, the SHRM Certification Exam Preview app, and the SHRM Certification Prep System®. The study guide includes much additional information about the exam and exam preparation strategies, and it also includes a set of practice items from a combination of the SHRM-CP and SHRM-SCP exams. The SHRM BASK reflects the blueprint for the SHRM-CP exam and should be used to develop your study plan. The SHRM Certification Exam Preview app is an additional resource for SHRM practice test questions that are broken down by the competencies listed in the SHRM BASK; it is a tool specifically designed to guide you to make the best application decision possible by getting a realistic preview of the two different exams so you apply for the exam that matches the type of work you do. Choosing the right exam to take is the most important decision you will make. The SHRM Certification Prep System is the comprehensive preparation tool offered by SHRM built upon the SHRM BASK.

In this SHRM-CP workbook, some of the key concepts that were introduced in the study guide are further explained. For example, a self-assessment for gauging strengths and development areas that are addressed in the exam was briefly introduced in the study guide; this is created in the current workbook to help with SHRM-CP exam preparation.

Thank you for allowing SHRM to embark on this journey with you toward SHRM-CP certification and beyond!

How to Apply

SHRM offers both certification exams during two testing windows every year. The first window is from May 1 to July 15, and the second window is from December 1 to February 15. Examinees choose where to take the exam in person at one of more than 500 Prometric testing centers across more than 180 countries.

After you have decided which exam to take, apply to take the exam on the SHRM website anytime between the Applications Accepted Starting Date and the Standard Application Deadline.

Examinees who apply by the **Early-Bird Application Deadline** and/or who are **SHRM members** receive a reduced exam fee. Note that exam applications apply to specific testing windows; after you have applied, transferring to the next testing window incurs an additional fee.

To learn more about the benefits of SHRM memberships, receive discounts on the SHRM Certification Prep System and the SHRM Certification exams, and much more, navigate to this link: https://www.shrm.org/membership.

To apply, you must:

1. Apply online (https://www.shrm.org/credentials/certification).
2. Create a user account.
3. Select the exam level you are eligible to take.
4. Complete the application form by agreeing to follow the terms of the SHRM Certification Candidate Agreement.
5. Pay the application fee.
6. After you receive your Authorization-to-Test (ATT) letter, schedule your exam directly through SHRM's test delivery vendor (https://www.prometric.com/shrm). Your ATT letter will outline several ways to schedule your exam and select your testing location.

ONLINE
Learn More about How to Apply for the Exam

https://www.shrm.org/credentials/certification/how-to-get-shrm-certified-process

SHRM-CP and SHRM-SCP Eligibility

SHRM Certified Professional (SHRM-CP)

- The SHRM-CP certification is intended for individuals who perform general HR or HR-related duties, or for currently enrolled students and individuals pursuing a career in Human Resource Management.
- Candidates for the SHRM-CP certification are not required to hold an HR title and do not need a degree or previous HR experience to apply; however, a basic working knowledge of HR practices and principles or a degree from an Academically Aligned program is recommended.
- The SHRM-CP exam is designed to assess the competency level of HR at the operational level. This level includes implementing policies, supporting day-to-day HR functions, or serving as an HR point of contact for staff and stakeholders.
- Refer to the SHRM BASK for detailed information on proficiency standards for this credential (i.e., Proficiency Indicators only for All HR Professionals).

SHRM Senior Certified Professional (SHRM-SCP)

- The SHRM-SCP certification is for individuals who have a work history of at least **three years performing strategic level HR or HR-related duties,** or for SHRM-CP credential holders who have held the credential for at least three years and are working in, or are in the process of transitioning to, a strategic level role.
- Candidates for the SHRM-SCP certification are not required to hold an HR title and do not need a degree to apply.
- The SHRM-SCP exam is designed to assess the competency level of those who engage in HR work at the strategic level. Work at this level includes duties such as developing HR policies and/or procedures, overseeing the execution of integrated HR operations, directing an entire HR enterprise, or leading the alignment of HR strategies to organizational goals.
- Applicants must be able to demonstrate that they devoted at least 1,000 hours per calendar year (Jan.–Dec.) to strategic-level HR or HR-related work.
  - More than 1,000 hours in a calendar year does not equate to more than one year of experience.
  - Part-time work qualifies as long as the 1,000-hour per calendar year standard is met.
  - Experience may be either salaried or hourly.
- Individuals who are HR consultants may demonstrate qualifying experience through the HR or HR-related duties they perform for their clients. Contracted hours must meet the 1,000-hour standard.
- Refer to the SHRM BASK for detailed information on proficiency standards for this credential (i.e., Proficiency Indicators for All HR Professionals and for Advanced HR Professionals).

Who Should Take the SHRM-CP® vs SHRM-SCP® Exam?

To help professionals—including those who are HR accountable for people management and organizational outcomes—determine which SHRM certification aligns with their career stage and responsibilities, it is essential to understand the target audience for each exam. Below is a comprehensive breakdown of job titles, professional profiles, and individuals with HR accountability who are best suited for the **SHRM-CP® (Certified Professional)** certification.

SHRM-CP® (Certified Professional)

The **SHRM-CP** is designed for professionals who are primarily engaged in operational roles, focusing on the implementation of policies, day-to-day HR functions, and supporting organizational HR initiatives. This certification is ideal for those who:

- Are early to mid-career HR professionals.
- Have responsibilities centered on **policy implementation, transactional HR activities, and employee relations**.
- Are building foundational HR expertise and competencies.

Job Title	Example Responsibilities	SHRM BASK Functional Area(s)	SHRM BASK Behavioral Competencies
HR Coordinator	Scheduling interviews, onboarding new hires, maintaining employee records, supporting HR programs	Talent Acquisition, Workforce Management, Employee Engagement & Retention	Communication, Relationship Management
HR Generalist	Administers benefits, handles employee relations, supports recruitment, manages compliance	Total Rewards, Employee & Labor Relations, Talent Acquisition	Business Acumen, Consultation, Ethical Practice
HR Specialist	Focuses on a specific HR area (e.g., benefits, recruitment, training)	Varies by specialty	Analytical Aptitude, Consultation
Talent Acquisition Coordinator	Coordinates job postings, interview scheduling, candidate communications	Talent Acquisition, Workforce Management	Communication, Inclusive Mindset, Relationship Management
Benefits Administrator	Manages employee benefits, handles enrollments, resolves benefit issues	Total Rewards, Risk Management	Analytical Aptitude, Ethical Practice, Business Acumen
Employee Relations Specialist	Handles employee complaints, investigates issues, supports conflict resolution	Employee & Labor Relations, Risk Management	Communication, Relationship Management, Ethical Practice
Compensation & Benefits Analyst	Analyzes salary data, benchmarks compensation, administers benefits	Total Rewards, Technology Management	Analytical Aptitude, Ethical Practice, Business Acumen

Actionable Guidance

- » Identify your job responsibilities to match with the SHRM BASK® areas and competencies above.
- » Focus your SHRM-CP® exam preparation on the functional areas and competencies most relevant to your daily work.
- » Use real-world scenarios from your role to deepen your understanding of exam concepts and apply them effectively.

By connecting your daily HR responsibilities to the SHRM BASK, your exam preparation is both practical and targeted, increasing your confidence and effectiveness as an HR professional.

If you believe the scope of your experience and responsibilities surpass those outlined above, we recommend consulting the SHRM-SCP Workbook and reviewing the SHRM-SCP Certification Exam Previews. SHRM Certification Exam Previews offer unique practice question sets to assess your readiness for either the SHRM-CP, SHRM-SCP, or a mixture to enhance your readiness and confidence ahead of test day. Whether you are looking for half-length exams or content domain specific offerings to enhance your areas of opportunity, SHRM is committed to your success, ensuring you have the tools to pick the exam that is right for you.

SHRM-SCP® (Senior Certified Professional)

The **SHRM-SCP** is intended for senior professionals who operate at a strategic level, influencing organizational direction, leading HR teams, and driving complex HR initiatives. This certification is best suited for those who:

- » Are mid to senior-level HR professionals.
- » Lead HR functions or departments.
- » Develop and execute **strategic HR initiatives**.
- » Influence organizational policy and decision-making.
- » Manage complex and multi-faceted HR projects.

Section 1

The SHRM-CP Exam Structure

Types of Exam Items

As defined in the *Ace Your SHRM Certification Exam* study guide and on the SHRM website, there are two general types of items on the SHRM-CP exam: (1) knowledge items (KIs) and foundational knowledge items (FKIs); and (2) situational judgment items (SJIs).

Knowledge items (including FKIs) are stand-alone multiple-choice items with four response options. Each KI tests a single piece of knowledge or application of knowledge.

Situational judgment items (SJIs) present realistic situations from workplaces throughout the world. Based on the scenario presented, SJIs ask test takers to consider the problem presented in the question within the context of the situation, and then select the best course of action to take. As with the KIs, these are multiple-choice items with four response options.

The distribution of items with respect to content and item type is essentially the same for both the SHRM-CP and SHRM-SCP exams. About half of the items on each exam are allocated across the three behavioral competency clusters, and the other half are allocated across the three HR knowledge domains. Approximately 40% of the items on each exam are situational judgment items, and the remainder are stand-alone items measuring either knowledge that is foundational to the behavioral competencies (10%) or HR-specific knowledge (50%).

Item Type

Situational Judgment (40%) HR-Specific Knowledge (50%)
Foundational Knowledge (10%)

Behavioral Competency Clusters	**HR Knowledge Domains**
Leadership (19%)	People (19%)
Business (17.5%)	Organization (18%)
Interpersonal (13.5%)	Workplace (13%)

Exam Items

The SHRM-CP exam consists of a total of 134 questions—110 of the questions are scored, and 24 of the questions are unscored. The purpose of unscored items is to gather data to determine if they are viable to become scored test items on future SHRM exams if they perform well. Think of unscored items like beta testing to gather tester data. While unscored items will not affect your overall score (getting unscored items incorrect will not count against you), it is important not to skip any questions.

The scored and unscored items are intermingled throughout the exam and are indiscernible from one another. This exam is broken into two equal halves, and each half contains 67 questions.

Each half is divided into three sections:

» **Section 1:** 20 KIs and FKIs (i.e., knowledge items for behavioral competencies)

» **Section 2:** 27 SJIs

» **Section 3:** 20 KIs and FKIs

Exam Timing

The total exam appointment time is four hours, which includes **3 hours and 40 minutes** of testing time for the exam itself. This equals approximately 98 seconds per question. It is important to use your time wisely.

It is critical to note that you will be unable to return to Exam Half 1 upon moving to Exam Half 2. Ensure that you have answered all of the questions to the best of your ability in Exam Half 1 before proceeding to the second half of the exam. There will be confirmatory prompts for you before transitioning to Exam Half 2.

The exam time is broken down into the following segments:

» **Introduction**, including agreeing to follow the terms of the Candidate Agreement and confidentiality reminders: 4 minutes

» **Tutorial**: 9 minutes

» **Exam Half 1**: Up to 1 hour and 50 minutes

» **Exam Half 2:** Up to 1 hour and 50 minutes

» **Post Exam Survey**: 6 minutes

There are a few transition screens throughout the exam that account for the remaining minutes.

Key Takeaway	Details
Two Main Item Types	• **KIs/FKIs**: Stand-alone multiple-choice questions testing HR knowledge and foundational competencies • **SJIs**: Scenario-based questions requiring selection of the best course of action in realistic workplace situations
Balanced Content Distribution	• **40% SJIs**: Focus on behavioral competencies • **60% KIs/FKIs**: 10% foundational knowledge, 50% HR-specific knowledge

Total Questions and Scoring	• **134 questions total**
	  • **110 scored** (contribute to final score)
	  • **24 unscored** (for future test development; indistinguishable from scored items)

Exam Structure and Sections	• **Two halves** (67 questions each)
	  • **Section 1**: 20 KIs/FKIs
	  • **Section 2**: 27 SJIs
	  • **Section 3**: 20 KIs/FKIs

Time Management Is Critical	• **4 hours total** • **3 hours 40 minutes** dedicated to answering questions • **~98 seconds per question**
Irreversible Progression	• **Cannot return to Exam Half 1 after moving to Half 2** • **Carefully review and complete all questions in the first half before proceeding**
Exam Segments and Flow	• **Introduction**: 4 minutes • **Tutorial**: 8 minutes • **Exam Half 1**: Up to 1 hour 50 minutes • **Exam Half 2**: Up to 1 hour 50 minutes • **Post Exam Survey**: 6 minutes • **Transition screens** account for remaining time

Section 2

Understanding the SHRM BASK

One of the most important things for you to understand as you prepare for the SHRM-CP exam is this:

> **All of the HR competencies and knowledge areas that are assessed on the SHRM-CP exam are detailed in the SHRM BASK.**

Conceptually, preparing for the SHRM-CP exam is not unlike preparing for the SHRM-SCP exam. Do not be fooled, however—they are completely different exams by design, emphasizing differences found in the **proficiency indicators** area of the SHRM BASK. Before deciding whether or not the SHRM-CP exam is right for you, it is critical to match your knowledge and experience with the key concepts and proficiency indicators with those in the SHRM BASK for **All HR Professionals** ensuring you feel comfortable and confident with the material.

The SHRM BASK can also be thought of as the blueprint for the SHRM-CP exam, much like an architect uses a blueprint to construct a building, testing programs use an 'exam blueprint' to build examinations. You can find the complete version of the SHRM BASK at:

> https://www.shrm.org/credentials/certification/exam-preparation/body-of-applied-skills-and-knowledge

While the SHRM-CP and SHRM-SCP share the same exam blueprint, the exams are designed to be completely distinct by way of using proficiency indicators to separate the knowledge, skills, and abilities required to address *operational-level* (SHRM-CP) HR duties and tasks versus *strategic-level* (SHRM-SCP) HR functions and responsibilities.

Important reminders as you prepare for the SHRM-CP exam:

- If something is not covered in the SHRM BASK, it is not eligible to be tested on the SHRM-CP exam. However, the SHRM BASK is an expansive document that covers many different areas, and given its breadth, you might not see everything that is presented in the SHRM BASK represented on the SHRM-CP exam in any given testing window.
- The SHRM BASK does not define your specific HR role, but rather the HR professional role in general. Therefore, it may cover more than your current or past HR roles.
- For individuals testing outside of the US, you are not held accountable for content covered in the US Employment Law & Regulations section of the SHRM BASK (Workplace content domain). Those items will be substituted with items from the Workplace domain.

Figure 2.1. The SHRM BASK Model

This workbook is designed to demystify the SHRM BASK, providing insights to aid your test preparation using the SHRM BASK as a study tool. In this section, we provide guidance on how to break the SHRM BASK into digestible segments to help you identify areas of strength and areas that you need to study more, ultimately creating a personalized study plan in preparation for the SHRM-CP exam.

Structure of the SHRM BASK

Simply reading through the SHRM BASK may be a daunting task due to the amount of information it contains. Before tackling the detail, it can be helpful to understand the structure and the elements comprising the model. Let's start with the basics.

» HR technical competency; divided into three content domains: *People*, *Organization*, and *Workplace*.

» Behavioral competency; divided into three content clusters: *Business*, *Interpersonal*, and *Leadership*.

The HR technical competency, **HR Expertise**, reflects the technical knowledge specific to the HR field for an HR professional to perform their role. **Behavioral competencies**, on the other hand, describe the knowledge, skills, abilities and other characteristics (KSAOs) that define proficient performance for a professional. They are more general in their applicability than the profession-specific technical competency. That is, many of these competencies may apply to different jobs, roles and professions but have been specifically defined in HR terms for the SHRM BASK.

In short, the HR Expertise technical competencies reflect what knowledge HR professionals apply on the job, and behavioral competencies reflect how they apply this knowledge.

Before we dig deeper, Figure 2.2 presents a high-level overview of the SHRM BASK structure including how Key Concepts (KC) or Proficiency Indicators (PI), or both, support the content area you are studying. Ensure you review the applicable Key Concepts and Proficiency Indicators, where applicable.

HR Expertise		
People	**Organization**	**Workplace**
» HR Strategy [KC/PI] » Talent Acquisition [KC/PI] » Employee Engagement & Retention [KC/PI] » Learning & Development [KC/PI] » Total Rewards [KC/PI]	» Structure of the HR Function [KC/PI] » Organizational Effectiveness & Development [KC/PI] » Workforce Management [KC/PI] » Employee & Labor Relations [KC/PI] » Technology Management [KC/PI]	» Managing a Global Workforce [KC/PI] » Risk Management [KC/PI] » Corporate Social Responsibility [KC/PI] » **US Employment Law & Regulations* [KC/PI]

Behavioral Competencies			
Leadership	**Leadership & Navigation** [KC]	**Ethical Practice** [KC]	**Inclusive Mindset** [KC]
	» Navigating the Organization [PI] » Vision [PI] » Managing HR Initiatives [PI] » Influence [PI]	» Personal Integrity [PI] » Professional Integrity [PI] » Ethical Agent [PI]	» Connecting I&D to Organizational Performance [PI] » Building the Infrastructure for an Inclusive and Diverse Culture [PI] » Ensuring Impartiality & Fairness [PI] » Cultivating an Inclusive and Diverse Culture [PI] » Operating in a Global Environment [PI]
Interpersonal	**Relationship Management** [KC]	**Communication** [KC]	
	» Networking [PI] » Relationship Building [PI] » Teamwork [PI] » Negotiation [PI] » Conflict Management [PI]	» Delivering Messages [PI] » Exchanging Organizational Information [PI] » Listening [PI]	
Business	**Business Acumen** [KC]	**Consultation** [KC]	**Analytical Aptitude** [KC]
	» Business and Competitive Awareness [PI] » Business Analysis [PI] » Strategic Alignment [PI]	» Evaluating Business Challenges [PI] » Designing HR Solutions [PI] » Advising on HR Solutions [PI] » Change Management [PI] » Service Excellence [PI]	» Data Advocate [PI] » Data Gathering [PI] » Data Analysis [PI] » Evidence-Based Decision-Making [PI]

** US Employment Law & Regulations content will only appear if you are testing within the US If you are testing elsewhere across the globe, those items will be substituted with other items from the Workplace HR Expertise domain.*

Figure 2.2. Overall Structure of the SHRM BASK

HR Expertise

The HR technical competency, HR Expertise, reflects the principles, practices, and functions of effective HR management. This competency is grouped into three main knowledge domains: *People, Organization, and Workplace*. The knowledge domains are further divided into 14 HR functional knowledge areas that describe the technical knowledge required to perform key HR activities.

- **People:** HR Strategy, Talent Acquisition, Employee Engagement & Retention, Learning & Development, and Total Rewards
- **Organization:** Structure of the HR Function, Organizational Effectiveness & Development, Workforce Management, Employee & Labor Relations, and Technology Management
- **Workplace:** Managing a Global Workforce, Risk Management, Corporate Social Responsibility, and US Law & Regulations

Each HR technical competency includes the following information:

- Definition of the functional areas.
- Key concepts describing the knowledge specific to the functional area.
- Proficiency indicators that apply to **All HR Professionals** (i.e., early career through executive career levels) as well as those that apply primarily to **Advanced HR Professionals** (i.e., senior and executive career levels).
  - Note that for the SHRM-CP, proficiency indicators for All HR Professionals are the key ones to attend to.

Behavioral Competencies

Behavioral competencies facilitate the application of technical knowledge. Successful HR professionals must understand and effectively perform the behavioral components of HR practice in addition to being in command of technical HR knowledge. The eight behavioral competencies are grouped into three clusters:

- **Business**: Business Acumen, Consultation, and Analytical Aptitude
- **Interpersonal**: Relationship Management and Communication
- **Leadership**: Leadership & Navigation, Ethical Practice, and Inclusive Mindset

Unlike the HR technical competency, each behavioral competency is further comprised of 3 to 5 sub-competencies for a total of 31 sub-competencies. Refer back to Figure 2.2 for an overview of the sub-competencies by their competency and cluster. For each behavioral competency, the following information is provided:

- Definition of the competency.
- Key concepts describing the foundational knowledge for the competency.
- Sub-competencies applicable to the competency, with definitions.
- Proficiency indicators that apply to all HR professionals as well as those that apply primarily to advanced HR professionals.
  - Similarly, proficiency indicators for all HR professionals are the key ones to attend to when preparing for the SHRM-CP exam.

Key Concepts and Proficiency Indicators

Structural Difference in the SHRM BASK

In addition to the what and how distinction between HR Expertise and behavioral competencies, another difference important to understanding the structure of the SHRM BASK focuses on where the key concepts and proficiency indicators are specified in the model.

As depicted in Figure 2.2, key concepts (KC) and proficiency indicators (PI) are specified for each knowledge area under **HR Expertise** technical competency (note the superscripts beside each knowledge area). However, behavioral competencies are structured differently in this regard: Key concepts are identified by behavioral competency, and proficiency indicators are identified by sub-competency.

The SHRM-CP certification focuses on the proficiency indicators identified for *All HR Professionals*, and the SHRM-SCP certification exam focuses only on the indicators identified for *Advanced HR Professionals*. Although the proficiency indicators relevant to all HR professionals clearly apply to advanced HR professionals at the senior and executive levels, they are not assessed directly on these indicators but are expected, on the job, to understand the concepts behind these functions, recognize their strategic importance, and be able to mentor junior employees in developing those behaviors.

Example of Parallel Proficiency Indicators

An example of this distinction can be seen by parallel proficiency indicators presented under the *Corporate Social Responsibility* (CSR) knowledge area within the Workplace functional knowledge domain.

- For **Advanced HR Professionals**: *Develops a CSR strategy that reflects the organization's mission and values.*
- For **All HR Professionals**: *Identifies and promotes opportunities for HR and the organization to engage in CSR activities that align with the organization's CSR strategy.*

Both proficiency indicators address the organization's CSR strategy. The *advanced* proficiency indicator highlights the higher-level organizational focus of developing this strategy, whereas the *all* proficiency indicator focuses on supporting the strategy by identifying and promoting opportunities in alignment with the organizational strategy.

How to Use the SHRM BASK for Studying

Now that you have an understanding of the overall structure of the SHRM BASK, the next step is to understand the format of exam items and how you can leverage the information in the SHRM BASK to help your preparation for the exam.

Item Types

Both the SHRM-CP and SHRM-SCP certification exams consist of two types of items: knowledge items (KIs)[1] and situational judgment items (SJIs).

Knowledge Items

KIs are stand-alone, multiple-choice items that test a single piece of knowledge or application of knowledge and make up 60% of the exam. Topics stem from the key concepts and proficiency indicators presented throughout the SHRM BASK.

Each KI assesses content knowledge according to one of four possible cognitive classifications, or levels of understanding or application, required to answer it:

» **Recall** items test the facts for that key concept such as defining a specific term or identifying a component of a theoretical model. This is the most basic type of KI.

» **Understanding** items requires the test taker to demonstrate their content knowledge by comprehending information, comparing two things, translating by applying knowledge or interpreting a concept to apply it to an example. These items assess the test taker's ability to recognize how HR concepts and terms manifest themselves in the workplace.

» **Problem-solving** items require test takers to apply their knowledge to develop a solution to a problem, which is something HR professionals do every day. To select the correct answer, the test taker must draw on their knowledge and understanding of many different concepts and strategies, which is more cognitively demanding than simply recalling the information.

» **Critical evaluation** items ask test takers to analyze information to predict an outcome. A competent HR professional uses the ability to predict outcomes to guide business strategy and execution.

---

1 The Ace Your SHRM Certification Exam: *The Official SHRM Study Guide for the SHRM-CP and SHRM-SCP Exams* references two types of knowledge items: KIs and foundational KIs (FKIs). KIs and FKIs follow the same structure; the only meaningful difference is that the content for a KI stem from a knowledge area under *HR Expertise*, whereas the content for an FKI stem from a *behavioral competency*. For this workbook, we refer to all knowledge items as KIs.

Situational Judgment Items

In comparison, SJIs test decision-making and judgment skills to identify the most effective response according to HR best practices, as established by HR subject matter experts. These items make up 40% of the exam, and involve three major components:

» A realistic situation (scenario) that is similar to what many HR professionals have likely experienced during their careers.

» Two to three questions addressing the scenario prompting test takers to solve a particular situation-specific issue in an action-oriented way.

» Four possible response options.

For example, while a KI may test your knowledge about different communication elements or techniques (for example, under the *Communication* behavioral competency), an SJI may ask you to identify the most effective way to communicate with leaders or with the organization given the circumstances presented in the scenario. In lieu of being able to assess each test taker's real-life response to the same situation, an SJI offers an opportunity for test takers to leverage their knowledge of key concepts, as well as HR best practices, to demonstrate how they might have responded to a similar real-life situation.

For more information about these item types, please refer to the SHRM Certification Prep System or *Ace Your SHRM Certification Exam.*

Creating a Study Plan from the SHRM BASK

As noted previously, simply reading the SHRM BASK all at once may be overwhelming and, as a result, not particularly helpful as a test preparation approach. Rather, the model needs to be consumed in smaller quantities. In the remainder of this section, we present an approach to examining the different components of the SHRM BASK to identify particular topics to study and further investigate during your test preparation.

First, we recommend picking a knowledge area or behavioral competency and sub-competency as a starting point. From there, you will leverage the key concepts and proficiency indicators to support the development of your customized study plan. You will repeat these steps for each knowledge area and sub-competency until you have completed your review of the SHRM BASK.

We present examples of applying this approach to a knowledge area and a behavioral competency and sub-competency in Section 3.

How to Study Key Concepts

Key concepts are the most straightforward component of the SHRM BASK with respect to identifying information to build your study plan. They specify the complete list of topics that will be covered on both the SHRM-CP and SHRM-SCP exams. Figuring out what you need to know and what is tested on the exam is an excellent place to start.

How to Study Proficiency Indicators

Proficiency indicators are a bit more complicated to use for building a study plan. They require more self-reflection and analysis than key concepts. As noted previously, proficiency indicators reflect what competent HR behavior and performance look like in practice. That is, they define high-level HR best practices according to their associated knowledge area or behavioral sub-competency. We present some recommended steps to analyze a proficiency indicator to help build your study plan.

Before we get started, you need to be clear which exam you are preparing for: SHRM-CP or SHRM-SCP. Remember that proficiency indicators are differentiated by which exam you will take. Indicators for all HR professionals will be assessed on the SHRM-CP exam, whereas indicators for advanced HR professionals, as well as all HR professionals, will be assessed on the SHRM-SCP exam.

Important Reminder

When reviewing the SHRM BASK, it is important to remember that the competency model reflects expectations for the HR profession in general and not your specific HR role or those of others in your organization. It is easy to get confused about what you do (or have done) in your career and what is considered proficient for the HR professional at your level in general.

Depending on your current job and past experiences, you may not have had the opportunity to perform or experience everything specified in the SHRM BASK, and that is okay. You don't have to have experience in all the areas presented to be eligible to take the exam. They are a guide as to what is expected of an HR professional at your level.

QUICK TIP
Recommended Steps to Identifying Key Concepts to Study

1. Review the list of key concepts for the particular functional knowledge area or behavioral competency of interest.
2. Ask yourself the following questions:
   » Which concepts do I know extremely well?
   » Which concepts am I only familiar with at a superficial level?
   » Which concepts do I have limited to no knowledge about?
3. Take note of with which key concepts you have only some or no familiarity. These are good targets to add to your study plan. It can also be useful to refresh on the key concepts that you think you know extremely well.
4. Think about how the key concept could be tested with KIs, according to the four cognitive levels (i.e., recall, understanding, problem-solving, and critical evaluation).
   » What are the facts about this key concept?
   » How would I demonstrate understanding of this key concept?
   » What types of problems could I be expected to solve that would rely on this key concept?
   » Can I predict outcomes under varying conditions?

QUICK TIP
Recommended Steps to Understanding Proficiency Indicators for the SHRM-CP exam

1. Review the proficiency indicators for *All HR Professionals* for a particular knowledge area or behavioral sub-competency of interest.
2. Ask yourself the following questions:
   » Which indicators resonate with experiences I have had during my HR career?
   » Which indicators am I familiar with because I have observed others perform them?
   » Which indicators am I unfamiliar with altogether?
3. As you did with the key concepts, take note of which proficiency indicators fall into each category. They will all require some further analysis to support your test preparation.
4. For each proficiency indicator, think about which key concepts are valuable for supporting the proficient performance of this indicator. Linking key concepts to proficiency indicators can aid your understanding of different applications for a key concept and scenarios you could encounter on the exam in KIs and SJIs.
5. For each proficiency indicator, identify the HR best practices for this indicator.
   » Think about what steps are involved in satisfying the proficiency indicator.
   » Identify any additional key concepts that you didn't initially select that could now be useful to study more closely. Go back to the recommended steps for using key concepts to determine if these need to go on your study plan list.
   » Consider that you may know the ways that you have handled this proficiency indicator in the past and these responses may have been effective for your given situation, but they may not actually reflect HR best practices.
   » Take note of the situations you have encountered or witnessed that have involved this proficiency indicator as these could be reflected on the exam.
   » Identify and add any HR best practices and proficiency indicators to your study plan list.
   » Can I predict outcomes under varying conditions?

<table>
<tr><th>Key Takeaway</th><th>Details</th></tr>
<tr><td>SHRM BASK Is the Exam Blueprint</td><td><ul><li>All HR competencies and knowledge areas assessed on the SHRM-CP exam are detailed in the SHRM Body of Applied Skills and Knowledge (BASK)</li></ul></td></tr>
<tr><td>Distinct Focus: SHRM-CP vs. SHRM-SCP</td><td><ul><li>Both exams use the same blueprint but assess different HR proficiency levels.<ul><li>SHRM-CP: Operational-level duties and tasks</li><li>SHRM-SCP: Strategic-level functions and advanced proficiency indicators</li></ul></li></ul></td></tr>
<tr><td>Comprehensive SHRM BASK Structure</td><td><ul><li>Two main competency types:<ul><li>HR Technical Competency (HR Expertise): 3 domains (People, Organization, Workplace) with 14 functional knowledge areas</li><li>Behavioral Competency: 3 clusters (Business, Interpersonal, Leadership) with 9 competencies and 33 sub-competencies</li></ul></li></ul></td></tr>
<tr><td>Key Concepts & Proficiency Indicators</td><td><ul><li>Key Concepts (KC): Foundational knowledge for each area/competency</li><li>Proficiency Indicators (PI): Expected behaviors and performance at different career levels</li><li>SHRM-CP: Focus on indicators for All HR Professionals</li></ul></td></tr>
<tr><td>Strategic Study Approach Using SHRM BASK</td><td><ul><li>Break down SHRM BASK into segments by functional area and competency</li><li>Identify strengths/gaps by reviewing KCs and PIs</li><li>Create a personalized study guide targeting unfamiliar or weak areas</li></ul></td></tr>
<tr><td>Global Applicability & Role Expectations</td><td><ul><li>SHRM BASK defines general HR expectations, not specific to personal job roles</li><li>Non-US test-takers: US Employment Law & Regulations content is replaced with other Workplace domain items</li></ul></td></tr>
</table>

Section 3

Using the SHRM BASK to Prepare for the SHRM-CP Exam

In this section, we take what we learned in Section 2 and apply it to the HR Expertise areas and behavioral competencies, selecting an example of each to highlight how you can leverage the SHRM BASK in your test preparation. This process will guide you through what you need to study to understand the nuance underlying the SHRM BASK.

HR Expertise Example: Organizational Effectiveness & Development

Using the recommended steps presented in Section 2, let's go through an example using the ***Organizational Effectiveness & Development*** knowledge area within the **Organization** knowledge domain. This technical knowledge area refers to the overall structure and functionality of the organization and involves (1) measurement of long- and short-term effectiveness and growth of people and processes and (2) implementation of necessary organizational change initiatives.

Note that the material presented under the HR Expertise technical competency will only be assessed with KIs.

Key Concepts

Because key concepts define testable content material, especially for KIs, we will start here and then move to proficiency indicators, selecting one example of each to examine more closely.

Step 1. Review Key Concepts

The first step is the most basic: Read the list of key concepts and the examples associated with the concepts. The key concepts for *Organizational Effectiveness & Development* are as follows:

» Group dynamics.

» Organizational design structures and approaches.

» Organizational analysis.

Step 2. Categorize Key Concepts According to Level of Familiarity

For each key concept, categorize them according to familiarity: extremely familiar, somewhat familiar (i.e., superficial knowledge), and limited to no familiarity. Make sure to review the associated examples as there may be some for which you may have more or less knowledge.

Step 3. Take Note of Any Key Concepts Requiring Additional Study

Any key concepts that fall into the latter two categories of somewhat or no familiarity are targets for further investigation and study. Identify these topics for your personal study plan. Recognize, of course, that a refresher review of any key concepts that you are already very comfortable with is a good idea to ensure your knowledge is up to date with the literature.

For this example, we will select the key concept of *group dynamics*.

» Examples of this key concept include *intergroup and intragroup; group formation; identity; cohesion; structure; influence on behavior; conflict; forming, storming, norming, and performing.*

Step 4. Identify How the Key Concept May Be Assessed with a KI

When studying the various key concepts, it is easy to stick to learning the facts about the concept such as the details associated with a particular theory or the steps involved in a process. Think about how you might use your knowledge to demonstrate your understanding, ability to solve situational problems, or predict outcomes.

Returning to our example, how might *group dynamics* be tested with a stand-alone KI?

To demonstrate how group dynamics can be assessed differently, Figures 3.1 and 3.2 present example KIs that reflect understanding and problem-solving, respectively.

Although both KI examples address group dynamics concepts and present example situations, the understanding item asks the test taker to assess the example and identify the theoretical term reflected in the example. The problem-solving KI, on the other hand, requires the test taker to take what they know about group dynamics and identify an effective solution to achieve the desired result of mitigating inter-unit conflict.

A manager is responsible for two teams that work in different locations. The manager wants to promote a more cohesive culture, but the teams continually disagree on key process issues. Which term does this exemplify?

A. Intergroup conflict

B. Personality differences

C. Power distance

D. Status differences

Key: C, Power distance

Description: This item reflects an understanding of the concept of power distance, which refers to power inequalities among individuals and groups. The item reflects understanding because it presents a situation that asks the test taker to identify the concept being depicted in the example situation.

Figure 3.1. Understanding KI for Group Dynamics

Following a recent merger, an operations executive informs the HR manager that key business units are in conflict over the value each group brings to the organization. Which activity should the HR manager recommend to the executive to address this?

A. Form a committee with leaders of different units to identify differences.

B. Hold a team-building activity with members from different units to form working partnerships.

C. Engage business unit leaders in direct communication to change the perceptions of other leaders.

D. Hold an all-hands meeting to promote a shared understanding of organizational values.

Key: D, Hold an all-hands meeting to promote a shared understanding of organizational values.

Description: This item is classified as problem-solving because it asks the test taker to assess the situation presented in the item and identify the best course of action given knowledge of group dynamics.

Figure 3.2. Problem-Solving KI for Group Dynamics

Proficiency Indicators

Proficiency indicators reflect HR best practices related to the HR technical competency or behavioral sub-competencies and can best be leveraged to identify context for situational prompts. As noted previously, they tend to be defined at the highest level of proficiency without dictating how the action can be accomplished. As a result, further analysis is required to support building a personal study plan.

Let's continue with our example of the functional knowledge area of *Organizational Effectiveness & Development* and apply the recommended process for one proficiency indicator.

Step 1. Review Proficiency Indicators for All HR Professionals

For the SHRM-CP exam, review the proficiency indicators listed for *All HR Professionals*. The proficiency indicators for *Organizational Effectiveness & Development* are as follows:

- Ensures that key documents and systems (examples include job postings, job descriptions, and performance management systems) accurately reflect workforce activities.
- Supports change initiatives to increase the effectiveness of HR systems and processes.
- Identifies areas in the organization's structures, processes, and procedures that need change.
- Recommends methods to eliminate barriers to organizational effectiveness and development.
- Collects and analyzes data on organizational performance and the value of HR initiatives to the organization.

Step 2. Categorize Proficiency Indicators According to Level of Familiarity

For each proficiency indicator, ask yourself the following questions regarding your familiarity with them as a result of your HR career to date:

» Which indicators resonate with experiences I have had during my HR career? (Extremely Familiar)

» Which indicators am I only familiar with because I have observed others perform them? (Somewhat Familiar)

» Which indicators am I unfamiliar with altogether? (Limited to No Familiarity)

Categorize the indicators according to familiarity: extremely familiar, somewhat familiar (i.e., superficial knowledge), and limited to no familiarity.

Step 3. Take Note of Any Proficiency Indicators Requiring Additional Study

Take note of which proficiency indicators fall into each familiarity category. Unlike key concepts, they will all require further analysis to support your test preparation.

Step 4. Link Proficiency Indicators to Key Concepts

For each proficiency indicator, think about which key concepts are valuable for supporting the proficient performance of this proficiency indicator. Linking key concepts to proficiency indicators can aid your understanding of different applications for a key concept and scenarios you could encounter on the exam.

For example, let's look at the proficiency indicator, *recommends methods to eliminate barriers to organizational effectiveness and development.* What key concepts are relevant to this indicator?

» *Group dynamics* assuming that there are issues with organizational cohesion and group performance.

» *Organizational design structures and approaches* because these could influence the methods that might be taken to eliminate structural barriers to effectiveness.

The problem-solving KI example presented in Figure 3.2 effectively demonstrates how a proficiency indicator can be leveraged to identify a context for applying a key concept. For convenience, we re-present the stem with an explanation of the linkage in Figure 3.3.

Step 5. Identify HR Best Practices

As written, there is a great deal of nuance in how a proficiency indicator can be accomplished or performed. Each proficiency indicator, as a result, can be broken down into lower-level components, each of which may have their own set of recommended best practices. Examining the lower-level steps or components will help you identify additional contextual situations that you may encounter on the exam, as well as additional key concepts that you may need to consider for review.

Item Stem	Linkage Explanation
Following a recent merger, an operations executive informs the HR manager that key business units are in conflict over the value each group brings to the organization. Which activity should the HR manager recommend to the executive to address this?	The item presents a situation and asks the test taker to recommend a method to eliminate an identified barrier to the organization's effectiveness. This item requires knowledge of the key concept (*group dynamics*) and directly links to the proficiency indicator (*recommends methods to eliminate barriers to organizational effectiveness and development*).

Figure 3.3. Key Concept Linkage Example: Technical Knowledge Area Proficiency Indicator

For each proficiency indicator

1. Think about how this proficiency indicator can be accomplished. What steps, factors, or other considerations are involved in satisfying the proficiency indicator?

   For this example proficiency indicator (*recommends methods to eliminate barriers to organizational effectiveness and development)* lower-level steps might include reviews organizational performance analysis for trends and patterns, consults with subject matter experts to identify potential solutions, or assesses merits of different solutions.

2. Identify any additional key concepts that you didn't initially select that could now be useful. Go back to the recommended steps for using key concepts to determine if these need to go on your study plan list.

   For example, if a lower-level step is reviewing an organizational performance report, you may want to add the key concept, organizational analysis, to your list of key concepts to study (if you haven't already).

3. Consider that you may know the ways that you have handled this proficiency indicator in the past, and these responses may have been effective for your given situation, but they may not actually reflect HR best practices.

4. Take note of the situations you have encountered or witnessed that have involved this proficiency indicator as these could be reflected on the exam.

5. Identify and add any HR best practices and proficiency indicators to your study plan list as needed.

Behavioral Competency Example: Relationship Management

Now let's do the same thing using a behavioral competency as the starting point, using *Relationship Management* from the *Interpersonal* cluster. Relationship Management is defined as the KSAOs needed to create and maintain a network of professional contacts within and outside the organization, to build and maintain relationships, to work as an effective member of a team, and to manage conflict while supporting the organization.

As evident in Figure 2.2, key concepts are specified at the behavioral competency level. As a result, we will begin with the behavioral competency when reviewing key concepts and eventually narrow down to a sub-competency when examining the proficiency indicators.

Key Concepts

As we did for HR Expertise, we will present how to use the recommended approach, focusing on one key concept for demonstration.

Step 1. Review Key Concepts

Read the list of key concepts and the examples associated with the concepts. The key concepts for *Relationship Management* are as follows:

- Types of conflict.
- Conflict resolution strategies.
- Negotiation tactics, strategies, and styles.
- Trust-building techniques.

Step 2. Categorize Key Concepts According to Level of Familiarity

For each key concept, categorize them according to familiarity: extremely familiar, somewhat familiar (i.e., superficial knowledge), and limited to no familiarity. Make sure to review the associated examples as there may be some for which you may have more or less knowledge.

Step 3. Take Note of Any Key Concepts Requiring Additional Study

Any key concepts that fall into the latter two categories of somewhat or no familiarity are targets for further investigation and study. Identify these topics for your personal study plan. Recognize, of course, that a refresher review of any key concepts that you are already very comfortable with is a good idea to ensure your knowledge is up to date with the literature.

For this example, we will select the key concept of *conflict resolution strategies.* Examples of this key concept include accommodation, collaboration, compromise, competition, and avoidance.

Step 4. Identify How the Key Concept May Be Assessed with a KI

Think about how you might use your knowledge to demonstrate your understanding and ability to solve situational problems, or predict outcomes.

Returning to our example, how might *conflict resolution strategies* be tested with a stand-alone KI?

To demonstrate how conflict resolution strategies can be assessed differently, Figures 3.4 and 3.5 present examples of KIs that reflect recall and problem-solving, respectively.

Which give-and-take decision-making process involves independent parties with different preferences? A. Diversity management B. Bargaining C. Conflict resolution D. Negotiation	**Key:** D, Negotiation **Description**: Negotiation by definition is a give-and-take process designed to help two or more parties come to a decision or resolution. For this item, the test taker is required to simply identify the term corresponding to the definition presented in the item stem and it is therefore classified as *recall*.

Figure 3.4. Recall KI for Conflict Resolution Strategies

A CEO wants to resolve a conflict between two executives without involving HR in the initial conversation. Which action should the HR manager suggest the CEO take to address this situation? A. Meet both employees in person to document the details for HR to review. B. Follow the company's code of conduct and conflict resolution policy. C. Refer the case to HR to explore options to resolve the interpersonal conflict. D. Consider mediation services to resolve the conflict.	**Key:** A, Meet both employees in person to document the details for HR to review. **Description:** This item presents a situation and requires the test taker to identify an effective response to resolve the problem. In this case, an effective first step, and recommended best practice, is for the CEO to meet with both employees to document the details carefully. The other response options may also be effective responses but do not address the details that the CEO would like to collect before involving HR at the outset.

Figure 3.5. Problem-Solving KI for Conflict Resolution Strategies

Although both KI examples address conflict resolution strategies, the recall item straightforwardly focuses on the definition of key terminology and does not require the test taker to do anything further than remember the information. The problem-solving KI, on the other hand, requires the test taker to take what they know about conflict resolution strategies and identify an effective solution to achieve the desired result before involving HR directly.

Proficiency Indicators

Continuing with *Relationship Management*, let's look at the proficiency indicators and follow the recommended approach identified in Section 2. However, as noted previously, remember that proficiency indicators are specified under sub-competencies. For this exercise, we will focus on the sub-competency of *Conflict Management*, which focuses on the management and resolution of conflicts by identifying areas of common interest among the parties in conflict.

Step 1. Review Proficiency Indicators for All HR Professionals

For the SHRM-CP exam, review the proficiency indicators listed for *All HR Professionals*. The proficiency indicators for *Conflict Management* are as follows:

» Resolves and/or mediates conflicts in a respectful, appropriate, and impartial manner, and refers them to a higher level when warranted.

» Identifies and addresses the underlying causes of conflict.

» Facilitates difficult interactions among employees to achieve optimal outcomes.

» Encourages productive and respectful task-related conflict and uses it to facilitate change.

» Serves as a positive role model for productive conflict.

» Identifies and resolves conflict that is counterproductive or harmful.

Step 2. Categorize Proficiency Indicators According to Level of Familiarity

For each proficiency indicator, ask yourself the following questions regarding your familiarity with them as a result of your HR career to date:

» Which indicators resonate with experiences I have had during my HR career? (Extremely Familiar)

» Which indicators am I only familiar with because I have observed others perform them? (Somewhat Familiar)

» Which indicators am I unfamiliar with altogether? (Limited to No Familiarity)

Categorize the indicators according to familiarity: extremely familiar, somewhat familiar (i.e., superficial knowledge), and limited to no familiarity.

Step 3. Take Note of Any Proficiency Indicators Requiring Additional Study

Take note of which proficiency indicators fall into each familiarity category. Unlike for key concepts, they will all require further analysis to support your test preparation.

Step 4. Link Proficiency Indicators to Key Concepts

For each proficiency indicator, think about which key concepts are valuable for supporting proficient performance of this indicator. Linking key concepts to proficiency indicators can aid your understanding of different applications for a key concept and scenarios you could encounter on the exam.

For the indicator, **resolves and/or mediates conflicts in a respectful and impartial manner, and refers them to a higher level when warranted**, for example, what key concepts are relevant to this indicator?

» *Types of conflict* because knowing the type of conflict may impact the method of resolution.

» *Conflict resolution strategies* because this indicator clearly focuses on the act of resolving the conflict.

» *Trust-building techniques* because effective conflict resolution typically involves employing the techniques presented as examples.

The problem-solving KI example presented in Figure 3.5 effectively demonstrates how a proficiency indicator can be leveraged to identify a context for applying a key concept. For convenience, we re-present the stem with an explanation of the linkage in Figure 3.6.

Item Stem	Linkage Explanation
A CEO wants to resolve a conflict between two executives without involving HR in the initial conversation. Which action should the HR manager suggest the CEO take to address this situation?	The item presents a situation and asks the test taker to recommend an initial step to address the situation before involving HR. This item requires knowledge of the key concept (conflict resolution strategies) and directly links to the proficiency indicator (resolves and/or mediates conflicts in a respectful and impartial manner, and refers them to a higher level when warranted).

Figure 3.6. Key Concept Linkage Example: Sub-Competency Proficiency Indicator

Behavioral sub-competency proficiency indicators can also provide situational context for SJIs. The next examples (Figure 3.7) showcase two SJIs based on the same scenario, both focusing on the sub-competency, Conflict Management.

Step 5. Identify HR Best Practices

This step is focused on doing a deeper dive into understanding the best practices associated with a proficiency indicator. Doing this analysis will help you identify additional contextual situations that you may encounter on the exam, as well as additional key concepts that you may need to consider for additional review.

For each proficiency indicator

1. Think about how this proficiency can be accomplished. What steps, factors, or other considerations are involved in satisfying the proficiency indicator?

   For this example indicator (resolves and/or mediates conflicts in a respectful, appropriate and impartial manner, and refers them to a higher level when warranted), lower-level steps might include: communicates with the parties in conflict to address and schedule meeting(s), identifies appropriate conflict resolution strategies, prepares for the conflict resolution meeting, and reviews policies regarding conflict management.

2. Identify any additional key concepts that you didn't initially select that could now be useful. Go back to the recommended steps for using key concepts to determine if these need to go on your study plan list.

   For example, your initial review of the proficiency indicator may not have signaled that the conflict required negotiation tactics but now you do. Therefore, you may want to add the key concept (negotiation tactics, strategies and styles) to your list of key concepts to study (if you haven't already).

3. Consider that you may know the ways that you have handled this proficiency indicator in the past and these responses may have been effective for your given situation, but they may not actually reflect HR best practices.

4. Take note of the situations you have encountered of witnessed that have involved this proficiency indicator as these could be reflected on the exam.

5. Identify and add any HR best practices and proficiency indicators to your study plan list, as needed.

<table>
<tr><th colspan="2">SJI Scenario</th></tr>
<tr><td colspan="2">The director at a telecommunications company receives several complaints about a manager who works on the director's team. The complaints allege that the manager demonstrates favoritism when interacting with direct reports. Moreover, the director has observed on multiple occasions that the manager does not get along well with the other managers on the team and is concerned that the manager consistently fails to meet performance objectives. The director has spoken to the manager on several occasions about all of these issues but has not observed any improvement. Both the director and manager approach the HR manager separately to complain about the other. The director complains about the manager's behaviors and poor performance, and the manager complains that the director is unfairly criticizing the manager's performance.</td></tr>
<tr><th colspan="2">Conflict Management SJI 1</th></tr>
<tr><td>Which action should the HR manager take to address the issue of the manager not getting along with the other managers?
A. Conduct a team-building event with all managers that highlights their shared goals.
B. Collect performance feedback from the other managers and privately share it with the manager.
C. Ask the director to be more supportive of the manager so that it sets a good example for the other managers.
D. Require all managers to meet regularly to discuss shared objectives and company goals.</td><td>Key: A, Conduct a team-building event with all managers that highlights their shared goals.</td></tr>
<tr><th colspan="2">Conflict Management SJI 2</th></tr>
<tr><td>Which action should the HR manager take to address the conflict between the director and the manager?
A. Suggest to the manager that explaining to the director how the manager feels may improve the situation.
B. Discuss with the manager the possibility of transferring to a new role under a different supervisor.
C. Meet with the manager and director separately to discuss the complaints and identify possible solutions.
D. Ask the director to share data with the HR manager that confirms the manager is not meeting performance objectives.</td><td>Key: C, Meet with the manager and director separately to discuss the complaints and identify possible solutions.</td></tr>
</table>

Figure 3.7. SJIs for Conflict Management

Key Takeaway	Details
Systematic Study Process	• **Review key concepts and proficiency indicators** for each HR Expertise area and behavioral competency. • **Categorize familiarity** (extremely, somewhat, limited/no familiarity). • **Target unfamiliar topics** for deeper study.
Connecting Concepts to Exam Questions	• **KIs:** Assess knowledge from recall to critical thinking using key concepts. • **SJIs:** Present scenarios requiring application of proficiency indicators and HR best practices.
Linking Key Concepts & Proficiency Indicators	• For each proficiency indicator, **identify relevant key concepts** that support proficient performance. • Understand how theoretical knowledge is applied in practical, exam-like situations.
Practice with Realistic Exam Items	• Use **practice items aligned with SHRM BASK** to familiarize with question formats and test-taking strategies. • Practice items preview exam structure but **do not predict final score or guarantee passing**.
Continuous Best Practice Identification	• For each proficiency indicator, **break down into actionable steps and HR best practices**. • Analyze lower-level components and contextual situations to anticipate exam scenarios.

Behavioral Competency Deep Dive	• When studying behavioral competencies (e.g., Relationship Management):
	  • **Review sub-competencies and proficiency indicators**.
	  • Link indicators to key concepts like conflict resolution, negotiation, trust-building.

Global and Contextual Relevance	• **SHRM BASK is globally applicable**. • **Non-US test-takers:** Certain items (e.g., US Employment Law & Regulations) are omitted. • Focus preparation on domains and competencies relevant to your exam context.

Section 4

The SHRM-CP Exam Blueprint

Not only does SHRM provide the potential content areas for the SHRM-CP exam in the SHRM BASK, SHRM also provides the actual breakdown of the numbers of exam items in the different content areas (Figure 4.1).

When measuring the three clusters of behavioral competencies, the exam includes close to equal representation from the different areas:

» **Leadership:** 19% of overall exam items.

» **Business:** 17.5% of overall exam items.

» **Interpersonal:** 13.5% of overall exam items.

In addition, for the HR knowledge domains, the People and Organization domains have more items than the Workplace domain. This difference is not surprising given the fact that Workplace only includes four functional areas, while People and Organization both include five functional areas.

» **People:** 19% of overall exam items.

» **Organization:** 18% of overall exam items.

» **Workplace:** 13% of overall exam items.

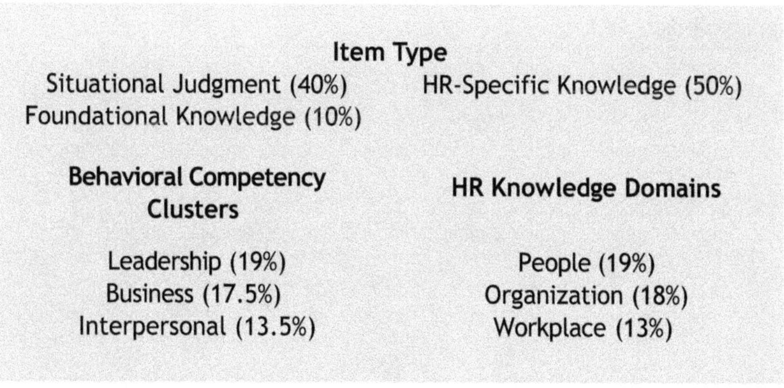

Figure 4.1. Distribution of Exam Items by Content and Exam Type

Self-Assessment for Your Exam Study Plan

Now that you have seen and started interacting with the SHRM BASK, you might feel a bit overwhelmed by the sheer volume of potential exam content. In fact, many SHRM-CP examinees are not sure what they should spend their time focused on and where they should start studying. Remember, the SHRM Certification Prep System is a robust option offering a comprehensive study package complete with pre-tests to assess your knowledge and identify gaps to provide a customized study plan based on your designated exam date.

To help diagnose your stronger and weaker areas and to direct your studying, we have put together this informal self-assessment for you. Note that this is not a true assessment of your knowledge but an informal resource you can use to determine where you need the most help and could benefit most in studying.

As you go through this assessment, try to be honest with yourself about your level of expertise. In many cases, you might not have a good understanding of your own knowledge level. That is okay and completely expected. If you are unsure of the meaning of terms, that is probably an indicator that you are not very knowledgeable in the area.

As a reminder, you can find the complete, complimentary, downloadable version of the SHRM BASK at:

https://www.shrm.org/credentials/certification/exam-preparation/bask

Instructions

Read the definition, sub-competencies (for behavioral competencies), key concepts, and proficiency indicators for all HR professionals. This will involve obtaining the full SHRM BASK and using the definitions and various pieces of information in it.

Rate the competencies and knowledge areas based on your level of expertise by placing an X in the appropriate box.

Section 1: Rate Competencies in Leadership Cluster

	Rate Your Level of Expertise		
	Low	Moderate	High
Leadership & Navigation			
Sub-competencies: » Navigating the organization » Vision » Managing HR initiatives » Influence			
Ethical Practice			
Sub-competencies: » Personal integrity » Professional integrity » Ethical agent			
Inclusive Mindset			
Sub-competencies: » Connecting I&D to Organizational Performance » Building the Infrastructure for an Inclusive and Diverse Culture » Ensuring Equity & Fairness » Cultivating an Inclusive and Diverse Culture » Operating in a Global Environment			

Section 2: Rate Competencies in Interpersonal Cluster

	Rate Your Level of Expertise		
	Low	Moderate	High
Relationship Management			
Sub-competencies: » Networking » Relationship building » Teamwork » Negotiation » Conflict management			
Communication			
Sub-competencies: » Delivering messages » Exchanging organizational information » Listening			

Section 3: Rate Competencies in Business Cluster

	Rate Your Level of Expertise		
	Low	**Moderate**	**High**
Business Acumen			
Sub-competencies: » Business and competitive awareness » Business analysis » Strategic alignment			
Consultation			
Sub-competencies: » Evaluating business challenges » Designing HR solutions » Advising on HR solutions » Change management » Service excellence			
Analytical Aptitude			
Sub-competencies: » Data advocate » Data gathering » Data analysis » Evidence-based decision-making			

Section 4: Rate Functional Areas in People Knowledge Domain

	Rate Your Level of Expertise		
	Low	**Moderate**	**High**
HR Strategy			
Talent Acquisition			
Employee Engagement & Retention			
Learning & Development			
Total Rewards			

Section 5: Rate Functional Areas in Organization Knowledge Domain

	Rate Your Level of Expertise		
	Low	**Moderate**	**High**
Structure of the HR Function			
Organizational Effectiveness & Development			
Workforce Management			
Employee & Labor Relations			
Technology Management			

Section 6: Rate Functional Areas in Workplace Knowledge Domain

	Rate Your Level of Expertise		
	Low	Moderate	High
Managing a Global Workforce			
Risk Management			
Corporate Social Responsibility			
US Employment Law & Regulations			

Scoring the Assessment

Based on your self-ratings of expertise for each behavioral competency or functional area, you can interpret the results based on your ratings of expertise.

Low Expertise = Study Most: These are areas where you have little to no expertise or experience. If you primarily support employee relations and employee engagement, you may need to study most in areas such as talent acquisition or inclusive mindset because you have little to no hands-on experience in this area.

Moderate Expertise = Study Some: These are areas where you have some expertise or experience, but you're not an expert. This could apply if you are a generalist with experience across many (or even most) competencies; you might have a surface-level knowledge of the competency, but you need to spend some time studying to better understand that competency outside of just your role or organization. If you used to work in a specific area but now perform a different set of job duties, this might apply too.

High Expertise = Review Only: These are the areas where you have the most expertise or experience. When you create your study plan, you don't want to spend too much time on these areas. Instead, you'll devote that time to studying the areas where you have more to learn. Note that these might be areas that you prefer to study or are most comfortable with. Because of this, you might have to fight the tendency to spend too much time in areas that you already know.

Interpreting the Assessment

You should now have 22 discrete ratings, one for each behavioral competency and functional area. Review your ratings and make notes about the terms, facts, and concepts that you need to learn or know more about so you can include them in your study plan.

It is important to review but not overstudy areas where your knowledge and familiarity with the content is already at a command-and-control level. Instead, focus your study efforts to improve your knowledge on the content with which you are least familiar. This means you should spend the majority of your study time on your study most areas, some time on your study some areas, and only a small amount of time on your review areas. Despite these recommendations, it is also important to note that the pass/fail decision for the exams are based on overall performance, rather than performance in each specific area. As a result, it is possible to pass the exam while performing rather poorly in a small number of subject areas.

After you have your completed self-assessment, group together the items on your checklist that you can study together to identify study blocks. As you sort items into groups, list the related terms and acronyms. After you've identified your study blocks, you'll have the outline for your study plan.

Also, we should note that the reference list at the end of the SHRM BASK has many relevant books and other resources that are relevant for learning more about these competencies and functional areas. Remember that it is not a comprehensive list, but these are resources that have been approved by SHRM for item writers to use when creating exam items.

Create a SMART Study Plan

A plan is when a *want to* becomes a *how to*.

After going through the self-assessment and gaining some understanding of the areas of the SHRM-CP where you might need more studying, you should commit to making a plan for preparing for the exam. Although you might be able to follow a generic or informal plan, we know that the act of planning and committing is important for a lot of people to do things that are difficult.

One of the main reasons to focus on the study plan and schedule is the importance of writing things down. You are much more likely to take a commitment more seriously if you document it in a clear way. As such, we encourage you to take advantage of this workbook and use the templates provided in Appendix 2.

Here's how to create a study schedule that will fit into your life:[1]

1. Figure out how many hours you will need to cover everything on your study checklist. SHRM research shows that you should plan on spending at least 80 hours of preparation for the exam—although some people will need significantly more preparation time.

2. Start with the results of the self-assessment and plan your study time accordingly. You should also consider factors such as the extent of your HR experience and how quickly you tend to learn.

3. Determine how much of your time is already committed elsewhere. This will vary greatly between people. You should consider the time you need for family, work, exercise, personal care, and social activities, along with downtime and time for the unexpected, such as illness or a heavier-than-usual workload.

4. Decide how many hours of study time you will have available each week before the exam. If you plan to either form or join a study group or take an exam prep course, identify how many hours each week you will need for those activities. Then divide the remaining time into study sessions.

---

1 Charles Glover, eds., *Ace Your SHRM Certification Exam: The Official SHRM Study Guide for the SHRM-CP® and SHRM-SCP® Exams*, 4th ed. (London, Kogan Page).

5. Determine a specific, achievable goal for each study session and identify the content you will study so you can achieve that goal. Keep in mind that you'll need more study time for some content than for others and build time into your schedule for practice exams so that you can assess what you are learning.

6. Develop a realistic study schedule that shows your study sessions by date and time, the goal for each session, and the content you'll focus on during that session. Try to use this to make a realistic plan for an average of six to eight hours of study per week. Please note that there is no expectation of studying every day; however, it will be a good idea for you to plan on at least three days per week of some studying.

7. Create a week-by-week calendar that includes your scheduled activities for each day during your study period. Include time for family and friends, work (including your commute), scheduled appointments (doctors, dentists, etc.), exercise, and study sessions, study group meetings, and exam prep courses (if any).

Get Started on Your Study Schedule

Now step back and review your calendar:

» How realistic is it?

» Did you leave time for meals and personal care, as well as some downtime so you can rest and relax?

» Did you leave buffer time in case of the unexpected?

If needed, go into your electronic calendar and set aside the time that you assigned to your studies.

Looking for next-level support in creating a study plan and sticking to it? As noted, the SHRM Certification Prep System will identify strengths and gaps in knowledge, allowing more time to prioritize the studying of weaker areas, and while maintaining your areas of strength.

A great feature in the SHRM Certification Prep System is the exam countdown calendar which will generate a customized study approach based on your selected exam date (and your proximity to it) top of mind, so you can plan your studies accordingly. You can pop in and out of the SHRM Certification Prep System when you have a little break, using your phone to access the many quizzes and lessons within the platform.

Key Takeaway	Details
Balanced Exam Item Distribution	• **Behavioral competencies:** Leadership (19%), Business (17.5%), Interpersonal (13.5%) • **HR Domains:** People (19%), Organization (18%), Workplace (13%)
Functional Area Weighting	• **People & Organization:** More items due to broader scope (5 functional areas each) • **Workplace:** Fewer items (4 functional areas)
Self-Assessment Drives Study Focus	• Use **SHRM BASK self-assessment** to identify strengths and gaps across competencies and domains • **Prioritize study efforts** where improvement is needed
Rating Scale for Expertise	• **Rate each area:** Low (study most), Moderate (study some), High (review only) • **Allocate study time:** Focus on low-rated areas, some time on moderate, minimal on high-rated areas
Customized Study Blocks	• **Group related competencies and functional areas** into study blocks • **List related terms and acronyms** for each block to ensure comprehensive coverage
SMART Study Planning	• **Specific:** Identify exact topics and goals • **Measurable:** Track hours and progress • **Achievable:** Set realistic weekly targets (6–8 hours/week) • **Relevant:** Focus on weaker areas • **Time-bound:** Use a week-by-week calendar and exam countdown
Leverage SHRM Certification Prep System & Resources	• **SHRM Certification Prep System:** Pre-tests, quizzes, exam countdown calendar for diagnosing gaps and tracking progress • **Reference materials:** Use approved resources listed in SHRM BASK to deepen understanding

Section 5

The SHRM-CP Twenty-Five-Item Practice Test

Introduction

This practice test includes 25 items that were previously used on the SHRM-CP exam. These are different items than the ones that are used in the official SHRM study guide, *Ace Your SHRM Certification Exam*, and only include SHRM-CP items.

Similar to the real exam, this practice test is divided into separate sections that are composed of either knowledge items or situational judgment items.

» **Section 1** contains a total of 7 knowledge and foundational knowledge items.

» **Section 2** contains 10 situational judgment items.

» **Section 3** contains a set of 8 knowledge and foundational knowledge items.

Because this practice test only contains 25 items, it is not entirely representative of the entire blueprint that is used to build the SHRM-CP and SHRM-SCP exams. However, it is generally set up to cover all of the areas in the blueprint. This practice test will give you a taste of how the questions are structured on the exam and allow you to practice your test-taking strategies as you answer them.

To get a better sense of the real exams, SHRM recommends that you take the practice items during a timed period. We suggest you allot one and a half minutes per question (37 minutes total) to gauge your ability to answer questions under the time constraints of the real exams.

One very important caution: do not assume that the ability to answer items on this 25-item practice test directly correlates to a passing score on the certification exam. This practice test is composed of less than half of the number of items on the SHRM-CP exams.

Additionally, the conditions in your at-home or in-office environment will not likely match the controlled environment in which a SHRM-CP exam is administered. For these reasons, the practice items are intended to give a preview of the structure and format of test questions. It is not appropriate to use these results to predict an outcome on your exam, and doing well on the practice test is not a guarantee of a passing result on your exam.

Additional information, including the answer key and rationales for the correct answers for knowledge and foundational knowledge items, appear at the end of the practice test. Answer keys are also provided for the situational judgment items, but rationales are not provided due to the inherent nature of how these items are developed. Situational judgment items require judgment and decision-making to address workplace incidents, rather than relying on policy or law. All response options are actions that could be taken to respond to the situation, but there is only one *most effective* response. The most effective response is determined by diverse groups of experienced SHRM-certified HR professionals from around the globe who rate the effectiveness of each response. They also use the proficiency indicators outlined by the eight behavioral competencies in the SHRM BASK. Scoring of the most effective response is only done if the group of HR experts agree that this is the best response of all given alternatives.

When answering the SJI questions, do not base your response on an approach that is specific to your organization. Rather, use your understanding of HR best practice, which is documented in the SHRM BASK, to select your response.

To further maximize your preparation for the exam, consider the SHRM Certification Prep System which includes full-length SHRM-CP and SHRM-SCP practice (timed) exams full of previously used test items along with learning modules and over 2,700 practice items to help fill in your knowledge gaps. The SHRM Certification Prep System is offered in a variety of formats—self-study and virtual or in-person seminars—and through partner universities that are authorized to teach the SHRM Certification Prep System content.

If you would like additional confidence that you are selecting the right exam level, SHRM Certification Previews offer unique quizzes complete with SHRM-retired exam questions. These mobile-friendly exam previews are designed to enhance your exam readiness in conjunction with the SHRM Certification Prep System, to aid you with the following options:

» **"Pick the Right Exam for You"**: Identifying which of the SHRM exams is right for you, with offerings complete with SHRM-CP and SHRM-SCP questions.

» **Half-length Quizzes**: Sixty-seven question quizzes, half the length of the exam, which cover the full range of the SHRM BASK pertaining to either the SHRM-CP or SHRM-SCP, respectively.

» **Domain-level Offerings**: Question sets dedicated solely to the individual HR Functional Areas: Workplace, Organization, People, or the Behavioral Clusters: Interpersonal, Business, Leadership, offering you a deep dive into one of the six content domains.

» **Item Type Offerings**: If you are looking to practice SJIs specifically, or KIs, we offer quizzes dedicated solely to those specific item types, covering a diverse range of content areas.

SHRM-CP Practice Test Questions

Section 1: This section is composed of seven (7) knowledge items.

1. An HR generalist wants to better understand employee turnover over the past five years. Which type of analytics helps to explain this type of data?

   A. Predictive

   B. Prescriptive

   C. Descriptive

   D. Normative

2. Which action should an HR manager take to most effectively encourage management to allow more people to work from home?

   A. Reduce incidences of micromanagement.

   B. Set realistic rules of engagement.

   C. Provide different communication tools.

   D. Offer spaces for remote social interactions.

3. Which is an HR manager's responsibility when helping employees resolve an ongoing conflict?

   A. Analyze the underlying issue to decide which employee to hold accountable.

   B. Organize a team-building activity to strengthen workplace morale.

   C. Select the appropriate disciplinary actions for the disagreeing employees.

   D. Facilitate open communication to lead to problem-solving strategies.

4. Which is the most effective practice for selecting employees to participate in a high-potential development program?

   A. Select employees who demonstrate learning agility.

   B. Select employees who are high-performing in their roles.

   C. Select employees that have long tenure with the company.

   D. Select employees who self-nominate.

5. Which is a response strategy to adverse risks in an organization?

   A. Avoid

   B. Accept

   C. Enable

   D. Share

6. A supervisor holds a team meeting to reassign an employee's duties to their co-workers before that employee takes an extended leave of absence. The supervisor does not disclose the reason for this leave to the team. Which ethical practice does this supervisor demonstrate?

   A. Transparency

   B. Confidentiality

   C. Fairness

   D. Privacy

7. Which is the first step an HR professional should take when organizing global talent activities?

   A. Identify the talent pool and key positions.

   B. Determine which region most of the talent will be managed.

   C. Create a consistent set of criteria that defines talent.

   D. Define what represents a key position within the organization.

Section 2: This section has ten (10) situational judgment items (SJIs).

The following scenario accompanies the next two items.

A sales associate informs the sales director about plans to accept a job offer with a different software company due to a lack of professional growth and work/life balance at the current company. The sales director knows the sales associate adds a strong work ethic, a high level of knowledge, and a great deal of experience to the sales associate's team. The sales director informs the CEO and the chief operating officer (COO) about the sales associate's desire to accept the job offer but wants to do everything possible to keep the sales associate in the company. The sales associate decides to stay with the company based on the feedback from the sales director but meets with the HR manager to discuss concerns about professional growth and work/life balance that many sales associates have. The HR manager identifies this as an opportunity to align plans for growing the company with changes to improve work for current sales associates. The HR manager begins formulating a proposal to improve work/life balance for sales associates while also preparing high-performing sales associates for changing roles as the company grows in number of sales and employees.

8. Which action should the HR manager take to best align talent recruitment and development with the company's plans for growth?

   A. Focus on developing sales-related competencies in sales associates to effectively achieve sales goals.

   B. Develop career path plans only for high-performing sales associates.

   C. Invest in innovative recruitment strategies for expanding the talent pool.

   D. Encourage employees to frequently ask for career development advice.

9. Which approach should the HR manager primarily use to present the proposal to the sales director?

   A. Identify the limitations the current company structure has on work processes and employees.

   B. Emphasize the importance of a realistic timeline for implementing the plan.

   C. Share direct quotes from employees about concerns regarding professional growth and work/life balance.

   D. Indicate the improved financial performance the proposal could bring to the company.

The following scenario accompanies the next three items.

The HR director and executive team of a midsize company meet to determine a plan of action to resolve the company's unexpected financial problems. In the previous year, the company projected extensive sales growth and hired many new employees. However, an unexpected downturn in the economy occurred and sales dropped significantly. During the meeting, the executive team and HR director determine the best course of action is a companywide reorganization that will include a reduction in force (RIF). The executive team believes the fairest way to determine which employees will be laid off is to require each department to reduce its total headcount by

10%. As part of the action plan, department managers will be asked to identify which employees to lay off to achieve the 10% departmentwide RIF within five business days. After the managers determine which employees will be impacted by the RIF, HR staff will create separation letters and severance packages. The HR director expresses concerns about the process and timeline because the HR director has a pre-planned vacation scheduled for the following week. In preparation for the HR director's absence, the HR director asks the HR staff to prepare a basic separation letter with a paragraph stating that full severance packages will be sent out within two weeks. The additional time will allow the HR director to work on the detailed severance packages after returning from vacation. As rumors of the RIF spread, employees begin expressing concerns about job stability to their managers.

10. A manager gets into a verbal altercation with a member of the executive team because the manager refuses to reduce the number of employees by more than 5%. How should the HR director resolve this conflict?

    A. Inform the manager that 10% of the manager's employees must be reduced based on company decision-making.

    B. Discuss with the executive team if an exception can be made for this manager.

    C. Schedule a meeting between the manager and the executive team to discuss the conflict.

    D. Tell the manager a decision will be made on the manager's behalf if the company's decision is not implemented.

11. The department managers believe every employee is essential and ask for the HR director's assistance in implementing the RIF. Which strategy should the HR director recommend for managers to determine which employees to include in the RIF?

    A. Present performance rating trends from the last three years.

    B. Evaluate each employee's tenure with the company.

    C. Assess each employee's number of professional development training hours.

    D. Rank employee importance based on job level.

12. The executive team requires the HR department to be readily available for employee questions after the official layoff announcement. Which is the best course of action for the HR director to take to maintain HR departmental reliability?

    A. Offer to be available by phone during the vacation to assist with any employee concerns.

    B. Select specific HR staff to address employees' RIF concerns during the vacation.

    C. Train managers to answer employee questions that HR would ordinarily address.

    D. Schedule an email apologizing for being unavailable during the RIF to affected employees.

The following scenario accompanies the next two items.

The CEO of a nonprofit wants to convert all of the organization's administrative functions to become fully digital in the next two years. To accomplish this, the CEO asks the HR director to partner with the leadership team to develop a digital transformation plan outlining strategic objectives that account for any impacts on company culture. The HR director suspects it will be challenging to get the leadership team to agree on a strategic plan for the transition because some members of the team are not in favor of becoming a fully digital organization. As part of the transition, the HR director advises the CEO that several employee positions will become obsolete and need to be terminated as a result. The funds originally used for these eliminated positions can then be reallocated to fund costs related to advancing technology, reskilling current employees, and hiring for new technology-focused positions. The CEO approves the plan to phase out the soon-to-be-obsolete positions and tells the HR director to inform the affected employees of their positions' eliminations within the next four months.

13. The HR director learns that a soon-to-be-terminated employee is attending virtual interviews on a company computer during lunch breaks, which is against company policy. Which action should the HR director take to address the policy violation?

    A. Advise the employee about the risks of using a company computer for personal purposes.

    B. Ask the employee to use a personal computer for interviews.

    C. Issue a companywide notice reminding all employees that company computers are not for personal use.

    D. Speak with the employee directly about what is acceptable regarding the use of company computers.

14. The HR director learns that additional technology will better support the HR administration of the digital transformation plan. Which action should the HR director take to determine which additional technology is best?

    A. Benchmark similar organizations to learn about their HR technology products.

    B. Invite HR technology companies to demonstrate their products' capabilities.

    C. Conduct an analysis to determine which HR functions would be better supported by additional technology.

    D. Schedule a meeting with leadership to determine the budget for additional HR technology products.

The following scenario accompanies the next three items.

For the past several years, a consulting company's IT department has experienced high turnover. During several exit interviews, departing IT employees stated that the IT director establishes unrealistic deadlines and instills fear when employees fail to meet them. The departing employees also claimed the IT director unfairly targets employees with different ethnic backgrounds than the IT director. The HR director shared the exit interview feedback and discussed the inclusivity and diversity issue with senior leadership and the IT director on multiple occasions. However, the IT director disagrees with the feedback and is not receptive to the HR director's suggestions. The HR director has concerns about the exit interview comments and investigates the claims against the IT director. While investigating the claims, the HR director notices most of the departed IT employees are from different ethnic backgrounds than the IT director. This appears to support the claims that the IT director may be demonstrating bias, which violates the company's inclusion and diversity (I&D) policy.

15. Senior leadership asks the HR director to address the IT employees' claims of unrealistic deadlines. Which action should the HR director take to resolve the complaints?

    A. Notify the IT employees that the IT director's deadlines are aligned with business needs.

    B. Distribute a memo to the IT employees informing them that the company is investigating the complaints.

    C. Send a companywide email encouraging employees to continue to report unrealistic deadlines.

    D. Conduct roundtables with IT employees to discuss their concerns about unrealistic deadlines.

16. The HR director believes the company's I&D policy is out of date. Which action should the HR director take first to update the policy?

    A. Compare the company's I&D policy to competitors' policies.

    B. Research HR best practices on I&D policies.

    C. Distribute an anonymous mandatory employee survey requesting policy change suggestions.

    D. Establish an internal policy committee to research and suggest updates.

17. Senior leadership and the HR director are worried that implicit bias may also occur in other departments. Which action should the HR director take to best ensure all staff are aware of the company's stance on I&D?

    A. Email all employees a memo about the company's I&D policy.

    B. Communicate that violations of the company's I&D policy will result in a formal investigation.

    C. Administer an interactive I&D training to all employees.

    D. Form a committee to hold companywide I&D-focused events.

Section 3: This section is composed of eight (8) knowledge items.

18. A hiring manager extends an offer for a software engineer position that requires an H-1B visa. Which step should the hiring manager take to initiate the visa process?

    A. Collect the fees from the candidate for the visa application process.

    B. File a petition with the government agency to issue a skilled worker's visa.

    C. Prepare the benefits equivalent package for the candidate.

    D. Contact the local employment office for a prevailing wage determination.

19. An HR director is examining the organization's current staff functions and skills as part of a skills gap analysis. Which is the next step for the HR director to take after analyzing the data?

    A. Consult with senior leaders on business goals.

    B. Determine a plan of action to close skills gaps.

    C. Implement strategies to close skills gaps.

    D. Collect additional observations of employee skills.

20. HR is tasked with transitioning from paper forms to an employee self-service HRIS. Which information is the employee accountable for to ensure accuracy?

    A. Reviewing individual tax reports and deduction statements.

    B. Updating position titles for promotions or department transfers.

    C. Submitting requests for scheduling changes to support time off.

    D. Contacting benefits administrators outside of open enrollment.

21. Which benefit should an HR manager recommend to an individual who is going through personal issues at home?

    A. Family medical leave

    B. Wellness program

    C. Disability insurance

    D. Employee assistance program

22. An employee reports being assigned less desirable work after lodging a harassment complaint against a supervisor. Which initial response should the HR manager take regarding the employee's report?

    A. Act as a mediator between the supervisor and employee to resolve the employee's original complaint.

    B. Tell the supervisor to stop assigning work to the employee to minimize additional interaction.

    C. Ask the supervisor why the employee might feel treated differently compared to other employees.

    D. Investigate the employee's claim to assess if retaliation occurred after the initial complaint.

23. A company is expanding its workforce and has published a new compensation plan, effective immediately. Which factor should a hiring manager communicate during compensation negotiations?

    A. Provide information about internal pay guidelines and its competitiveness with the external market.

    B. Discuss salary range upfront, merit increases, and bonus guidelines to include career advancement opportunities.

    C. Focus on how the job description and performance expectations align with the salary.

    D. Compare the differences between the previous and new compensation policy to highlight the advantages of the new plan.

24. A company is going through a merger and senior leadership updates the organization's values. How should the HR manager ensure internal staff learn the new values?

    A. Reference the values during onboarding and orientation.

    B. Present and discuss the values openly in meetings.

    C. Add the values to the company website and job descriptions.

    D. Ask values-based questions in annual performance reviews.

25. Which is the most effective technique for promoting a collaborative and interactive corporate culture?

    A. Establish a clear organizational hierarchy.

    B. Build a common work ethic among employees.

    C. Collect 360-degree feedback for performance reviews.

    D. Orient new employees to company policies and procedures.

Appendix 1

The SHRM-CP Practice Test Answers

Question Number	Item Data		Rationale
1	Domain	BUSINESS	"Descriptive" is correct. Descriptive analytics is the appropriate method for understanding employee turnover over the past five years, as it summarizes historical data to identify patterns and trends. This approach enables the HR generalist to clearly see what has happened and establish a foundation for further analysis.
	Sub-competency	BUSINESS ACUMEN	
	Difficulty	Somewhat Hard	
	Key	C	
2	Domain	WORKPLACE	"Set realistic rules..." is correct. This is correct because this strategy gives management confidence that goals will be met and thus reduces their anxiety against remote working.
	Sub-competency	MANAGING A GLOBAL WORKFORCE	
	Difficulty	Somewhat Hard	
	Key	B	
3	Domain	INTERPERSONAL	"Facilitate open communication..." is correct. Facilitating communication between the two employees will allow the manager to serve as a mediator. In doing so the manager can assist in identifying the root cause of the conflict, allow both employees to feel "heard" and provide the manager with the opportunity to model/suggest problem-solving strategies.
	Sub-competency	RELATIONSHIP MANAGEMENT	
	Difficulty	Easy	
	Key	D	
4	Domain	PEOPLE	"Select employees who demonstrate..." is correct. This is correct because workers that possess learning agility are able to apply lessons from previous experiences to new conditions they encounter.
	Sub-competency	LEARNING & DEVELOPMENT	
	Difficulty	Hard	
	Key	A	
5	Domain	WORKPLACE	"Avoid" is correct. Threats can be categorized into opportunities (positive risk) or threats (adverse risks). Risk responses to adverse risks, or threats, are: escalate, avoid, accept, transfer, or mitigate.
	Sub-competency	RISK MANAGEMENT	
	Difficulty	Somewhat Hard	
	Key	A	
6	Domain	LEADERSHIP	"Confidentiality" is correct. This is correct because the supervisor is protecting the employee's privacy by not disclosing why the employee is going on leave.
	Sub-competency	ETHICAL PRACTICE	
	Difficulty	Easy	
	Key	B	

Question Number	Item Data		Rationale
7	Domain	ORGANIZATION	"Identify the talent pool..." is correct. This is correct because organizations define talent as the top 10–15% of staff within the organization.
	Sub-competency	STRUCTURE OF THE HR FUNCTION	
	Difficulty	Somewhat Hard	
	Key	A	
8	Domain	LEADERSHIP	Situational judgment items (SJIs) require the examinee to think about what is occurring in the scenario and decide which response option identifies the most effective course of action. Other response options may be something you could do to respond in the situation, but SJIs require thinking and acting based on the best of the available options. Do not base your answer on your organization's approach to handling the situation but, rather, answer based on what you know should be done according to best practice. Panels of SHRM-certified subject matter experts rate the effectiveness of each response option, and the "best" answer is derived by statistical analysis of those expert opinions.
	Sub-competency	LEADERSHIP & NAVIGATION	
	Difficulty	Somewhat Hard	
	Key	A	
9	Domain	BUSINESS	
	Sub-competency	CONSULTATION	
	Difficulty	Somewhat Easy	
	Key	D	
10	Domain	INTERPERSONAL	
	Sub-competency	RELATIONSHIP MANAGEMENT	
	Difficulty	Somewhat Easy	
	Key	C	
11	Domain	BUSINESS	
	Sub-competency	ANALYTICAL APTITUDE	
	Difficulty	Somewhat Easy	
	Key	A	
12	Domain	BUSINESS	
	Sub-competency	CONSULTATION	
	Difficulty	Easy	
	Key	B	
13	Domain	LEADERSHIP	
	Sub-competency	ETHICAL PRACTICE	
	Difficulty	Easy	
	Key	D	
14	Domain	LEADERSHIP	
	Sub-competency	LEADERSHIP & NAVIGATION	
	Difficulty	Somewhat Easy	
	Key	C	

Question Number	Item Data		Rationale
15	Domain	INTERPERSONAL	
	Sub-competency	COMMUNICATION	
	Difficulty	Easy	
	Key	D	
16	Domain	LEADERSHIP	
	Sub-competency	INCLUSIVE MINDSET	
	Difficulty	Somewhat Easy	
	Key	B	
17	Domain	LEADERSHIP	
	Sub-competency	INCLUSIVE MINDSET	
	Difficulty	Easy	
	Key	C	
18	Domain	WORKPLACE	"Contact the local employment office..." is correct. This is the very first step once the determination has been made that a H-1B visa should be procured. An H-1B visa makes sense in this scenario because it is a highly skilled/degree requiring job.
	Sub-competency	US EMPLOYMENT LAW & REGULATIONS	
	Difficulty	Hard	
	Key	D	
19	Domain	ORGANIZATION	"Determine a plan of action..." is correct. By examining the organization's current staff functions and skills, the HR director will determine what the skills gaps are and come up with strategies to close skills gaps. Companies often can address skills gaps by encouraging employees to pursue continuing education and certifications and by promoting cross-training within the enterprise. However, in some specialized areas, HR professionals may need to recruit talent from outside the organization.
	Sub-competency	WORKFORCE MANAGEMENT	
	Difficulty	Somewhat Easy	
	Key	B	
20	Domain	ORGANIZATION	"Reviewing individual tax reports and deductions..." is correct. This is an example of the payroll function often included in self-service systems. Payroll mistakes attract the loudest complaints, which makes it even more important to devolve some responsibility for its accuracy to the individual likely to complain. If an employee needs to change their withholdings for taxes, that should be their responsibility to manage.
	Sub-competency	TECHNOLOGY MANAGEMENT	
	Difficulty	Somewhat Hard	
	Key	A	
21	Domain	PEOPLE	"Employee assistance program" is correct. EAPs are a free service offered through many employers and address a wide variety of issues for employees and their families. EAPs provide assistance with financial issues, personal issues, family counseling, etc.
	Sub-competency	TOTAL REWARDS	
	Difficulty	Easy	
	Key	D	

Question Number	Item Data		Rationale
22	Domain	ORGANIZATION	"Investigate the employee's claim..." is correct. This is correct because it is best practice to obtain additional information and know both sides of the situation when a report is made before proceeding with any additional actions.
	Sub-competency	EMPLOYEE & LABOR RELATIONS	
	Difficulty	Easy	
	Key	D	
23	Domain	PEOPLE	"Discuss salary range upfront..." is correct. The objective is to deliver a comprehensive compensation package where potential new hires can visualize career and professional development at the company. ("Focus on the value of the entire deal: responsibilities, location, travel, flexibility in work hours, opportunities for growth and promotion, perks, support for continued education, and so forth. Think not just about how you're willing to be rewarded but also when.")
	Sub-competency	TALENT ACQUISITION	
	Difficulty	Hard	
	Key	B	
24	Domain	WORKPLACE	"Present and discuss the values..." This is correct, and the best answer, because if it's brought up during meetings and discussed openly, it's a great place to explain, clarify, and answer questions. It creates better alignment, causing a shared understanding.
	Sub-competency	CORPORATE SOCIAL RESPONSIBILITY	
	Difficulty	Easy	
	Key	B	
25	Domain	PEOPLE	"Build a common work ethic..." is correct. This is correct because in order to foster healthy company culture, all employees regardless of their role should have common interest in the success of the company.
	Sub-competency	EMPLOYEE ENGAGEMENT & RETENTION	
	Difficulty	Somewhat Hard	
	Key	B	

Appendix 2

Twelve-Week Study Schedule Template

We have provided a set of study schedule templates to guide your SHRM-CP exam preparation. Please use these spaces to create your plan and write it down.

Planned Test Date with Prometric: ____________________

Study Week 1: ________________

Weekly Goal: This week, I will...

____

____

____

____

	Planned Time	Study Focus
Sunday		
Monday		
Tuesday		
Wednesday		
Thursday		
Friday		
Saturday		

Study Week 2: ________________

Weekly Goal: This week, I will...

____

____

____

____

	Planned Time	Study Focus
Sunday		
Monday		
Tuesday		
Wednesday		
Thursday		
Friday		
Saturday		

Study Week 3: ________________

Weekly Goal: This week, I will...

____

____

____

____

	Planned Time	Study Focus
Sunday		
Monday		
Tuesday		
Wednesday		
Thursday		
Friday		
Saturday		

Study Week 4: ________________

Weekly Goal: This week, I will...

___

___

___

___

	Planned Time	Study Focus
Sunday		
Monday		
Tuesday		
Wednesday		
Thursday		
Friday		
Saturday		

Study Week 5: ________________

Weekly Goal: This week, I will...

____

____

____

____

	Planned Time	Study Focus
Sunday		
Monday		
Tuesday		
Wednesday		
Thursday		
Friday		
Saturday		

Study Week 6: ______________

Weekly Goal: This week, I will...

____

____

____

____

	Planned Time	Study Focus
Sunday		
Monday		
Tuesday		
Wednesday		
Thursday		
Friday		
Saturday		

Study Week 7: ________________

Weekly Goal: This week, I will...

____

____

____

____

	Planned Time	Study Focus
Sunday		
Monday		
Tuesday		
Wednesday		
Thursday		
Friday		
Saturday		

Study Week 8: ________________

Weekly Goal: This week, I will...

____

____

____

____

	Planned Time	Study Focus
Sunday		
Monday		
Tuesday		
Wednesday		
Thursday		
Friday		
Saturday		

Study Week 9: ________________

Weekly Goal: This week, I will...

____

____

____

____

	Planned Time	Study Focus
Sunday		
Monday		
Tuesday		
Wednesday		
Thursday		
Friday		
Saturday		

Study Week 10: ________________

Weekly Goal: This week, I will...

____

____

____

____

	Planned Time	Study Focus
Sunday		
Monday		
Tuesday		
Wednesday		
Thursday		
Friday		
Saturday		

Study Week 11: ______________

Weekly Goal: This week, I will...

____

____

____

____

	Planned Time	Study Focus
Sunday		
Monday		
Tuesday		
Wednesday		
Thursday		
Friday		
Saturday		

Study Week 12: ________________

Weekly Goal: This week, I will...

____

____

____

____

	Planned Time	Study Focus
Sunday		
Monday		
Tuesday		
Wednesday		
Thursday		
Friday		
Saturday		

Index

Looking for another book?

Explore our award-winning books from global business experts in Human Resources, Learning and Development

Scan the code to browse

www.koganpage.com/hr-learning-development

ISBN: 9781398627734

www.koganpage.com